The Bacon Cookbook for Cooking the Best Meals Ever

The Perfect Recipes for Bacon Lovers

BY

MOLLY MILLS

Copyright © 2019 by Molly Mills

License Notes

No part of this book may be copied, replicated, distributed, sold or shared without the express and written consent of the Author.

The ideas expressed in the book are for entertainment purposes. The Reader assumes all risk when following any guidelines and the Author accepts no responsibility if damages occur due to actions taken by the Reader.

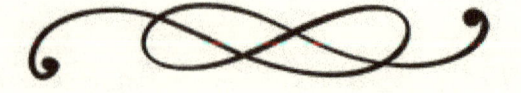

An Amazing Offer for Buying My Book!

Thank you very much for purchasing my books! As a token of my appreciation, I would like to extend an amazing offer to you! When you have subscribed with your e-mail address, you will have the opportunity to get free and discounted e-books that will show up in your inbox daily. You will also receive reminders before an offer expires so you never miss out. With just little effort on your part, you will have access to the newest and most informative books at your fingertips. This is all part of the VIP treatment when you subscribe below.

SIGN ME UP: *https://molly.gr8.com*

Table of Contents

Delicious Bacon Recipes 7

Recipe 1: Swiss and Bacon Stuffed Meatloaf 8

Recipe 2: Bacon and Spinach Smothered Penne Pasta . 10

Recipe 3: Bacon and Water Chestnut Rolls 12

Recipe 4: Easy Bacon and Tomato Grilled Cheese Sandwiches 14

Recipe 5: Healthy Apple and Bacon Soup 16

Recipe 6: Barbequed Bacon Wrapped Shrimp............... 19

Recipe 7: Fried Cabbage Stuffed with Bacon and Garlic 21

Recipe 8: Easy Blue Cheese Dip with Bacon 23

Recipe 9: Classic Potato and Bacon Soup 25

Recipe 10: Chicken and Bacon Stuffed Dumplings 27

Recipe 11: Roasted Chicken and Bacon 30

Recipe 12: Bacon Style Quiche Tarts 32

Recipe 13: Pork Medallions Wrapped in Bacon 34

Recipe 14: Bacon and Pineapple Packed Burgers.......... 36

Recipe 15: Feta Cheese and Bacon Stuffed Chicken Breasts 38

Recipe 16: Gouda and Bacon Stuffed Pork Chops 40

Recipe 17: Blue Cheese and Bacon Stuffed Chicken Breasts 42

Recipe 18: Grilled Bacon Wrapped Jalapenos 45

Recipe 19: Cheese and Bacon Stuffed Potato Rounds.. 47

Recipe 20: Bacon and Ranch Pasta Salad 49

Recipe 21: Bacon Wrapped Hamburgers 51

Recipe 22: Classic Chicken and Bacon Shish Kabobs.. 53

Recipe 23: Healthy BLT Salad.. 56

Recipe 24: Delicious BLT Dip.. 58

Recipe 25: Delicious Bacon and Cheddar Deviled Eggs
.... 60

About the Author 62

Don't Miss Out! 64

Delicious Bacon Recipes

AAAAAAAAAAAAAAAAAAAAAAAAAAAAAAAAAAAAAAAAAAAA

Recipe 1: Swiss and Bacon Stuffed Meatloaf

If you are a huge fan of meatloaf, then I know for a fact that you are going to love this recipe. With this recipe you will add some brown ground beef, Swiss cheese and hearty bacon and bake it to perfection. Once you get a taste of it I know you are going to love it.

Serving Sizes: 6 Servings

Preparation Time: 1 Hour and 35 Minutes

List of Ingredients:

- 12 Ounces of Bacon, Raw and Finely Chopped
- 1 Onion, White in Color, Small in Size and Finely Chopped
- 5 Mushrooms, Button Variety and Finely Chopped
- 1 ½ Pounds of Ground Beef, Extra Lean Variety
- 1 Egg, Large in Size and Beaten
- ¼ Cup of Milk, Evaporated Variety
- 6 Ounces of Swiss Cheese, Finely Shredded and Evenly Divided

- ½ Cup of Crumbs, Corn Flake Variety

AAAAAAAAAAAAAAAAAAAAAAAAAAAAAAAAAAAAAAAAAAAA

Instructions:

1. The first thing you want to do is preheat your oven to 350 degrees.

2. Then cook your bacon in a large sized skillet place over medium to high heat. Cook until thoroughly brown in color. Once browned remove and drain on a plate lined with paper towels. Once cooled, crumble.

3. Next use a large sized bowl and combine your remaining ingredients together along with your cooked bacon. Stir to combine. Place into your meat loaf pan.

4. Place into your oven to bake for the next hour and then remove from the oven. Top with cheese and return to your oven to cook for the next 5 minutes or until your cheese is completely melted. Remove and allow to cool before serving.

Recipe 2: Bacon and Spinach Smothered Penne Pasta

If you are looking to make a meal in relatively short time and that is healthy, this is the perfect recipe for you. Feel free to pair this dish alongside any other entrée that you wish to make a truly filling meal that you will love.

Serving Sizes: 4 Servings

Preparation Time: 25 Minutes

List of Ingredients:

- 1 Pack of Penne Pasta, Uncooked
- 2 Tablespoons of Olive Oil, Extra Virgin Variety and Evenly Divided
- 6 Slices of Bacon, Finely Chopped
- 2 Tablespoons of Garlic, Minced
- 1 Can of Tomatoes, Finely Diced
- 1 Bunch of Spinach, Fresh, Rinsed and Roughly Torn

AAAAAAAAAAAAAAAAAAAAAAAAAAAAAAAAAAAAAAAAAAAAAAAA

Instructions:

1. First bring a large size pot of water to a boil over high heat. Once the water is boiling add in your pasta and cook until tender. This should take about 8 to 10 minutes.

2. Then cook your bacon in a large sized skillet place over medium to high heat. Cook until thoroughly brown in color. Once browned remove and drain on a plate lined with paper towels. Once cooled, crumble.

3. Add your cooked bacon, tomatoes and garlic back into your skillet and cook thoroughly for the next 2 minutes.

4. Next place your spinach into a colander and drain your cooked pasta over the top of it until it wilts. Transfer this to a large size serving bowl and toss with your tomato mixture and some olive oil until thoroughly combined. Serve right away.

Recipe 3: Bacon and Water Chestnut Rolls

Here is yet another easy bacon recipe to prepare and I know you are going to love it. These rolls, while covered in some mayo and hot sauce, makes for a filling and delicious treat that you are going to want to make over and over again.

Serving Sizes: 24 Servings

Preparation Time: 1 Hour and 10 Minutes

List of Ingredients:

- 1 Can of Chestnuts, Water Variety and Cut into Halves
- ½ Pound of Bacon, Finely Sliced and Cut in Half
- ¼ cup of Mayo, Your Favorite Kind
- ½ Cup of Brown Sugar, Light and Packed
- ¼ Cup of Chili Sauce, Tomato Based

AAAAAAAAAAAAAAAAAAAAAAAAAAAAAAAAAAAAAAAAAAAAAA

Instructions:

1. The first thing you want to do is preheat your oven to 350 degrees.

2. Wrap each of your chestnuts with a slice of bacon and place them into a medium sized baking dish, making sure the seam side is facing down.

3. Place into your oven to bake for the next 30 minutes or until your bacon is crispy. Remove and drain the grease.

4. Then use a small sized bowl and combine your remaining ingredients together until thoroughly combined. Pour this mixture over your cooked chestnut rolls and return to your oven to bake for another 30 minutes. Remove and allow to cool slightly before serving.

Recipe 4: Easy Bacon and Tomato Grilled Cheese Sandwiches

This is a great grilled cheese sandwich recipe that everybody in your household will fall in love with. These are so delicious that even your kids will love. While this recipe is simple to make, the use of bacon and tomato truly makes this is a wonderful dish to make for lunch or dinner.

Serving Sizes: 4 Servings

Preparation Time: 15 Minutes

List of Ingredients:

- 4 Slices of Bacon, Thick Cut
- ¼ Cup of Butter, Soft
- 8 Slices of Bread, White in Color
- 8 Slices of Cheese, American Variety
- 8 Slices of Tomato, Fresh

AAAAAAAAAAAAAAAAAAAAAAAAAAAAAAAAAAAAAAAAAAAAA

Instructions:

1. Use a large sized deep skillet and cook up your bacon over medium heat until thoroughly brown in color. Drain and set your bacon aside.

2. Then use a separate large sized skillet placed over medium heat.

3. While your skillet is heating up spread your butter evenly on all of your slices of bread. Then place them butter side down in your skillet. Top off with your cheese, tomato slices and bacon slices. Cover with your remaining slice of bread, making sure the butter side is out.

4. Fry your sandwiches on both sides until gold in color.

Recipe 5: Healthy Apple and Bacon Soup

This is a rich and flavorful soup that makes for the ultimate soothing soup dish during the cold winter months. Feel free to top this soup with some shredded mozzarella cheese to make it truly delicious.

Serving Sizes: 8 Servings

Preparation Time: 45 Minutes

List of Ingredients:

- 5 Slices of Bacon, Thick Cut
- 1 tablespoon of Olive Oil, Extra Virgin Variety
- ½ an Onion, White in Color and Finely Chopped
- 2 teaspoons of Garlic, Minced
- 2 Cups of Beef Broth, Homemade Preferable
- 1 Can of Beans, Pinto Variety
- 1 Can of Tomatoes, Italian Style and Stewed Variety
- 2 Stalks of Celery, Finely Chopped
- 1 Bay Leaf, Fresh
- 1 Apple, Medium in Size and Sliced Thinly
- ½ Cup of Wine, Red in Color
- Dash of Salt, For Taste
- Dash of Pepper, For Taste

AAAAAAAAAAAAAAAAAAAAAAAAAAAAAAAAAAAAAAAAAAAAAAAA

Instructions:

1. First cook your bacon in a large sized skillet place over medium to high heat. Cook until thoroughly brown in color. Once browned remove and drain on a plate lined with paper towels. Once cooled, crumble.

2. Then heat up some oil in a large size saucepan placed over medium heat and add in your onion and garlic. Cook for the next 5 minutes or until tender. Add in your next five ingredients and stir to thoroughly combine. Bring this mixture to a boil and then reduce the heat to low.

3. Using a separate small sized saucepan placed over medium heat, add in your apple and red wine and allow to cook until soft. Mix this into your tomato mixture and stir to combine.

4. Season your soup with the dash of salt and pepper and continue to simmer until thoroughly piping hot. Remove and serve right away.

Recipe 6: Barbequed Bacon Wrapped Shrimp

If you want to enjoy something a bit spicy, yet that makes one of the most delicious meals that you will ever taste, this is the perfect recipe for you. This can easily be served as an entrée that feeds two or that can serve as an appetizer. Either way I know you are going to love it.

Serving Sizes: 3 Servings

Preparation Time: 50 Minutes

List of Ingredients:

- 16 Shrimp, Large in Size, Peeled and Deveined
- 8 Slices of Bacon, Thick Cut
- Some Barbecue Seasoning, According to Your Taste

AAAAAAAAAAAAAAAAAAAAAAAAAAAAAAAAAAAAAAAAAAAA

Instructions:

1. The first thing that you will want to do is preheat your oven to 450 degrees.

2. Then wrap up your shrimp with a half slice of bacon, making sure to secure it with a toothpick to hold it in place. Continue until all of your shrimp has been wrapped.

3. Then use a large sized baking pan and line it with some aluminum foil. Place your wrapped shrimp onto the pan and season generously with your barbecue season. Allow to sit for at least 15 minutes.

4. After this time place into your oven to bake for the next 10 to 15 minutes. Remove and allow to cool slightly before serving. Enjoy!

Recipe 7: Fried Cabbage Stuffed with Bacon and Garlic

This is an easy side dish recipe that even the pickiest of eaters will fall in love with. This dish is packed full of beautiful colors and is just as appetizing as it looks.

Serving Sizes: 6 Servings

Preparation Time: 1 Hour and 15 Minutes

List of Ingredients:

- 6 Slices of Bacon, Thick Cut
- 1 Onion, Large in Size and Finely Diced
- 2 Cloves of Garlic, Minced
- 1 Head of Cabbage, Large in Size, Cored and Roughly Sliced
- 1 tablespoon of Salt, For Taste
- 1 teaspoon of Black Pepper, For Taste
- ½ teaspoons of Onion, Powder
- ½ teaspoons of Garlic, Powder
- 1/8 teaspoons of Paprika

Instructions:

1. Add your bacon into a large sized stockpot and cook your bacon in a large sized skillet place over medium to high heat. Cook until thoroughly brown in color. Once browned remove and drain on a plate lined with paper towels. Once cooled, crumble.

2. Then add in your onion and garlic and continue to cook until your onion starts to caramelize. This should take about 10 minutes.

3. Add in your cabbage and continue to cook for the next 10 minutes and season with your spices.

4. Reduce your heat to low and continue to cook for the next 30 minutes. Remove from heat and serve right away.

Recipe 8: Easy Blue Cheese Dip with Bacon

Even if you aren't really a fan of blue cheese dip, this is one type of recipe that you will fall in love with. Feel free to serve this dish with some vegetables or French bread for the tastiest results.

Serving Sizes: 14 Servings

Preparation Time: 1 Hour

List of Ingredients:

- 7 Slices of Bacon, Thick Cut
- 2 Cloves of Garlic, Peeled and Minced
- 1 Pack of Cream Cheese, Soft
- ¼ Cup of Half and Half
- 4 Ounces of Blue Cheese, Crumbled
- 2 Tablespoons of Chives, Fresh and Roughly Chopped

AAAAAAAAAAAAAAAAAAAAAAAAAAAAAAAAAAAAAAAAAAAAAAAAA

Instructions:

1. The first thing you want to do is place your bacon into a large sized skillet place over medium to high heat or until brown in color. Once browned remove and drain on a plate lined with paper towels. Once cooled, crumble.

2. Then cook your garlic and your bacon grease for at least one minute. After this time remove and set aside.

3. Next preheat your oven to 350 degrees. While your oven is heating up place your cream cheese and half and half into a medium sized bowl and beat with an electric mixer until thoroughly blended. Add in your remaining ingredients and stir to combine.

4. Transfer to a medium-size baking dish and cover with aluminum foil.

5. Place in the oven to bake for the next 30 minutes or until light brown in color.

Recipe 9: Classic Potato and Bacon Soup

If you are looking for a hearty and filling soup, then this is the perfect recipe for you. This makes a great tasting soup dish that you can make whenever you are feeling under the weather or when you just want to warm yourself up on a cold winter's night.

Serving Sizes: 6 Servings

Preparation Time: 50 Minutes

List of Ingredients:

- 6 Slices of Bacon, Thick Cut
- 1 ½ teaspoons of Olive Oil, Extra Virgin Variety
- ½ Cup of Onion, Finely Chopped
- ½ Cup of Carrots, Fresh and Finely Chopped
- 1 Stalk of Celery, Finely Chopped
- 4 Cups of Chicken Broth, Low in Fat and Low in Sodium
- 4 Cups of Potatoes, Cut into Cubes
- 1/8 teaspoons of Cayenne Pepper

- ½ Cup of Cheddar Cheese, Finely Shredded
- ½ teaspoons of Salt, For Taste

AAAAAAAAAAAAAAAAAAAAAAAAAAAAAAAAAAAAAAAAAAAA

Instructions:

1. First cook your bacon in a large sized skillet place over medium to high heat. Cook until thoroughly brown in color. Once browned remove and drain on a plate lined with paper towels. Once cooled, crumble.

2. Add your oil into a large size saucepan and add in your next three ingredients. Cook for the next 3 to 4 minutes or until your vegetables are soft.

3. Add in your next three ingredients and stir to combine. Bring your mixture to a boil and then reduce the heat to low and continue cooking for the next 10 to 15 minutes or until your potatoes are tender.

4. Stir in your cheese and add in your cooked bacon. Stir to combine. Feel free to season with some more salt and pepper and serve right away.

Recipe 10: Chicken and Bacon Stuffed Dumplings

If you are looking for something easy to make and that will leave you feeling incredibly satisfied, this is the perfect recipe for you. Regardless of where your tastes lie, I know you are going to love this recipe.

Serving Sizes: 8 Servings

Preparation Time: 50 Minutes

List of Ingredients:

- 3 Slices of Bacon, Thick Cut
- 3 Potatoes, Large in Size, Peeled and Finely Diced
- 1 Onion, Finely Sliced
- 4 Chicken Breasts, Boneless, Skinless and Diced Finely
- 3 Cups of Chicken Broth, Homemade Preferable
- 1 teaspoon of Poultry Seasoning
- Dash of Salt, For Taste
- Dash of Pepper, For Taste
- 1 Can of Kernel Corn, Whole, Drained and Rinsed
- 3 Cups of Half and Half
- 1 ½ Cups of Biscuit Mix
- 1 Cup of Milk, Whole

AAAAAAAAAAAAAAAAAAAAAAAAAAAAAAAAAAAAAAAAAAAAAA

Instructions:

1. The first thing you want to do is cook your bacon in a large sized skillet place over medium to high heat. Cook until thoroughly brown in color. Once browned remove and drain on a plate lined with paper towels. Once cooled, crumble.

2. Then add your next three ingredients into your bacon grease and cook for the next 15 minutes, making sure to stir constantly. Add in your next four ingredients and stir to combine. Add in your corn and stir again. Allow to cook for the next 15 minutes over a simmering heat.

3. Then add in your half and half and bring your mixture to a boil before adding in your bacon.

4. Use a medium sized bowl and combine your biscuit mix with your whole milk and stir well until you have a sticky and thick dough. Drop at least one tablespoon at a time of your dough into your boiling mixture until all of your dough has been added. Continue cooking for the next 10 minutes while uncovered, and then cover with a lid and continue cooking for the next 10 minutes.

5. After this time remove and serve right away

Recipe 11: Roasted Chicken and Bacon

Who doesn't love the taste of bacon? Well, with this great tasting dish you can enjoy the savory taste of chicken without all of the hassle in making it. The bacon that you will use in this recipe will help to baste your chicken as it cooks, making the end results as delicious as you can dream it to be.

Serving Sizes: 6 Servings

Preparation Time: 2 Hours and 30 Minutes

List of Ingredients:

- 2 Tablespoons of Butter, Soft
- 1, 4 Pound Chicken, Whole
- Dash of Salt, For Taste
- Dash of Pepper, For Taste
- 1 teaspoon of Thyme, Dried
- 2 Carrots, Fresh and Cut into Small Pieces
- Dash of Paprika, For Taste
- 8 Slices of Bacon, Thick Cut
- 2 Cups of Beef Broth, Homemade Preferable

AA

Instructions:

1. First heat up your oven to 450 degrees.

2. Next rub butter all over your chicken and season with a generous amount of salt, pepper, and thyme. Fill up your chicken cavity with your carrots and tie the legs together with some string.

3. Then place your chicken into a large sized roasting pan with the breast side up. Lay your bacon strips over the top of your chicken and secure with a few toothpicks. Sprinkle with a dash of paprika and pour your beef broth inside of the pan.

4. Place your chicken into your oven to roast for the next 15 minutes and then reduce your heat to 350 degrees. During this time baste your chicken with some broth and continue to cook for the next hour and 15 minutes. Make sure that you baste your chicken at least every 15 minutes during the cooking process.

5. Remove your bacon and continue to cook your chicken for at least 15 more minutes. Remove and serve right away with your bacon slices. Enjoy.

Recipe 12: Bacon Style Quiche Tarts

These tasty tarts make for the most perfect appetizer dish that you can serve to a large group of people. These tarts are easy to make and will satisfy an entire group. I guarantee that once your friends get a taste of these tarts, they will be begging for me.

Serving Sizes: 10 Servings

Preparation Time: 40 Minutes

List of Ingredients:

- 5 Slices of Bacon, Thick Cut
- 1 Pack of Cream Cheese, Soft
- 2 Tablespoons of Milk, Whole
- 2 Eggs, Large in Size and Beaten
- ½ Cup of Swiss Cheese, Finely Shredded
- 2 Tablespoons of Onions, Green in Color and Finely Chopped
- 1 Can of Biscuit Dough, Flaky and Refrigerated

AAAAAAAAAAAAAAAAAAAAAAAAAAAAAAAAAAAAAAAAAAAAAAA

Instructions:

1. The first thing you want to do is preheat your oven to 375 degrees. While your oven is heating up grease a muffin pan generously with some cooking spray.

2. Then cook your bacon in a large sized skillet place over medium to high heat. Cook until thoroughly brown in color. Once browned remove and drain on a plate lined with paper towels. Once cooled, crumble.

3. Then use a medium sized bowl and combine your next three ingredients. Use an electric mixer and beat thoroughly until smooth and consistency. Then add in your Swiss cheese and green onions and beat again to combine. Set this mixture aside.

4. Next separate your dough into 10 individual biscuits and press them into the bottom of your muffin pan. Sprinkle half of your bacon on top of the dough and spoon at least two tablespoons of your cream cheese mixture on top.

5. Place into your oven to bake for the next 20 to 25 minutes or until golden brown and color. Remove from oven and allow to cool before serving.

Recipe 13: Pork Medallions Wrapped in Bacon

This is another great tasting entrée dish that you can make for the holiday season. Wrapped in bacon you can rest assured that these pork medallions are packed full of delicious flavor that you won't be able to resist.

Serving Sizes: 4 Servings

Preparation Time: 40 Minutes

List of Ingredients:

- 8 Slices of Bacon, Thick Cut
- 1 tablespoon of Garlic Powder
- 1 teaspoon of Salt, For Taste
- 1 teaspoon of Basil, Dried
- 1 teaspoon of Oregano, Dried
- 2 Pounds of Pork, Tenderloin Variety
- 2 Tablespoons of Butter, Soft
- 2 Tablespoons of Olive Oil, Extra Virgin Variety

AAAAAAAAAAAAAAAAAAAAAAAAAAAAAAAAAAAAAAAAAAAAAAAA

Instructions:

1. The first thing you want to do is preheat your oven to 400 degrees.

2. While your oven is heating up cook your bacon in a large sized skillet place over medium to high heat. Cook until thoroughly brown in color. Once browned remove and drain on a plate lined with paper towels. Once cooled, crumble.

3. Then take a small sized bowl and combine your next 4 ingredients together until thoroughly combined. Set aside.

4. Wrap each of your pork tenderloins with at least one strip of bacon and use a toothpick to secure it in place. Then dip your medallions into your seasoning mix.

5. Melt your butter and oil together in a large sized skillet and place over medium to high heat. Cook for at least 4 minutes on each side and remove after this time.

6. Place your skillet into your oven and bake for the next 17 to 20 minutes or until your pork is no longer pink in the middle. Remove and serve right away.

Recipe 14: Bacon and Pineapple Packed Burgers

This is one of my all-time favorite hamburger recipes out there and I know once you get a taste of these I know they will become your favorite too. These are great burgers to make during the summer holiday or whenever you are looking for something sweet to eat.

Serving Sizes: 4 Servings

Preparation Time: 25 Minutes

List of Ingredients:

- 2 Pounds of Beef, Ground and Lean
- ½ Cup of Barbecue Sauce, Your Favorite Kind
- 1 Can of Pineapple, Finely Sliced
- 8 Slices of Bacon, Thick Cut

AAAAAAAAAAAAAAAAAAAAAAAAAAAAAAAAAAAAAAAAAAAAAAAA

Instructions:

1. The first thing you want to do is preheat your grill to medium-high heat.

2. Then use a large sized bowl and mix together your hamburger meat and your BBQ sauce, making short to season with some salt and pepper. Mixed with your hands until evenly combined.

3. Shape your meat mixture into patties and place a slice of pineapple on top of each patty. Top with your bacon strips and secure each with a toothpick.

4. Then brush your grill with some oil and place your burgers on to the grill. Cook while covered until your burgers are fully cooked through. Remove from grill once done and serve with hamburger buns. Enjoy.

Recipe 15: Feta Cheese and Bacon Stuffed Chicken Breasts

Here is yet another stuffed chicken breast dish that I know you are going to drool over. These particular chicken breasts are packed full of bacon and feta cheese and make for the ultimate dinner meal that will satisfy all of your taste buds.

Serving Sizes: 4 Servings

Preparation Time: 45 Minutes

List of Ingredients:

- 8 Tablespoons of Olive Oil, Extra Virgin Variety
- 2 teaspoons of Lemon Juice, Fresh
- 4 Cloves of Garlic, Crushed
- 1 tablespoon of Oregano, Dried
- Dash of Salt, For Taste
- Dash of Pepper, For Taste
- 4 Chicken Breasts, Skinless and Boneless Variety
- 4 Slices of Feta Cheese
- 4 Slices of Bacon, Fried and Fully Drained

AAAAAAAAAAAAAAAAAAAAAAAAAAAAAAAAAAAAAAAAAAAAAAAA

Instructions:

1. The first thing you want to do is preheat your oven to 350 degrees.

2. While your oven is heating up use a small sized bowl and combine your first five ingredients together until evenly mixed.

3. Stuff your chicken breast with your feta cheese and at least one slice of bacon and secure with a toothpick.

4. Place your chicken into a generously greased baking dish and pour your mixture over the top.

5. Bake uncovered in your oven for the next 30 to 35 minutes or until your chicken fully cooked through. Remove and serve right away.

Recipe 16: Gouda and Bacon Stuffed Pork Chops

These are easy and elegant pork chops to serve when you are looking for something special and classy to serve. Keep in mind that when you need to stuff your pork chops, ensure that you do not stuff them 100% full.

Serving Sizes: 2 Servings

Preparation Time: 35 Minutes

List of Ingredients:

- 2 Ounces of Gouda Cheese, Smoked and Finely Shredded
- 4 Slices of Bacon, Fully Cooked and Crumbled
- ¼ Cup of Parsley, Fresh and Roughly Chopped
- 1/8 teaspoons of Black Pepper, For Taste and Ground
- 2 Pork Chops, Center Cut and with Bone-In
- 1 teaspoon of Olive Oil, Extra Virgin Variety
- ¼ teaspoons of Salt, For Taste
- Dash of Black Pepper, For Taste

AAAAAAAAAAAAAAAAAAAAAAAAAAAAAAAAAAAAAAAAAAAAAAAA

Instructions:

1. The first thing you want to do is preheat an outdoor grill over medium heat.

2. Then use a small sized bowl and combine your first four ingredients together until thoroughly combined.

3. Lay your pork chops onto a cutting board and slice a deep pocket in the center of each pork chop. Stuff your cheese mixture into each pocket and close off with a toothpick. Brush your pork with some oil and season with a dash of salt and pepper.

4. Then brush your grill with some oil and grill your pork chops for the next 5 to 8 minutes on each side or until every pork chop is fully cooked through. Remove and serve remove right away.

Recipe 17: Blue Cheese and Bacon Stuffed Chicken Breasts

This is actually a recipe I made up while trying to figure out what to do with some leftovers I had stored in my fridge. Feel free to add or leave out ingredients according to your taste.

Serving Sizes: 4 Servings

Preparation Time: 45 Minutes

List of Ingredients:

- 8 Slices of Bacon, Thick Cut
- 4 Chicken Breasts, Cut into Halves, Skinless and Boneless Variety
- 1 Pack of Spinach, Frozen, Thawed and Roughly Chopped
- 1 Cup of Blue Cheese, Crumbled
- 2 Tablespoons of Flour, All Purpose Variety
- 1/8 teaspoons of Black Pepper, For Taste
- ¼ teaspoons of Salt, For Taste
- 2 Tablespoons of Olive Oil, Extra Virgin Variety

AA

Instructions:

1. The first thing that you will want to do is cook your bacon in a large sized skillet place over medium to high heat. Cook until thoroughly brown in color. Once browned remove and drain on a plate lined with paper towels. Set aside for later use.

2. Then preheat your oven to 350 degrees.

3. While your oven is preheating use a medium sized bowl and stir together your blue cheese and fresh spinach. Crumble your bacon and add into this mixture and stir to evenly combine.

4. Lay out of your chicken breasts on a clean service and cut a slice into each chicken forming a pocket. Stuff with your spinach make sure and secure with a toothpick.

5. Then mixed together your flour and dash of salt and pepper on a large size dinner plate and roll your chicken in the flour to coat.

6. Next heat up some oil in a large size skillet and set over medium to high heat. Brown each piece of your chicken until lightly browned and color. Remove and transfer to a generously greased baking dish. Cover with aluminum foil.

7. Place into your oven to bake for the next 30 minutes or until your chicken is fully cooked through. Remove and serve right away with your desired side dish. Enjoy.

Recipe 18: Grilled Bacon Wrapped Jalapenos

These delicious jalapenos are stuffed full of soft cream cheese, wrap with savory bacon and are grilled to perfection. These are great snacks to make during your next family barbecue and will surely leave your family wanting more.

Serving Sizes: 6 Servings

Preparation Time: 20 Minutes

List of Ingredients:

- 6 Jalapeno Peppers, Fresh, cut in Half and Seeded
- 1 Pack of Cream Cheese, Soft
- 12 Slices of Bacon, Thick Cut

AAAAAAAAAAAAAAAAAAAAAAAAAAAAAAAAAAAAAAAAAAAAAA

Instructions:

1. The first thing you want to do is preheat an outdoor grill over medium heat.

2. Spread your cream cheese into each jalapeno half and wrap each with a slice of bacon. Secure your peppers with a few toothpicks.

3. Place onto your grill and cook just until your bacon is crispy. Remove and serve right away.

Recipe 19: Cheese and Bacon Stuffed Potato Rounds

These are a great side dish to serve alongside a whole chicken or a few steaks. These potato rounds combine the perfect combination of potatoes, bacon and shredded cheese. For the tastiest results serve these rounds with a spoonful of sour cream.

Serving Sizes: 4 Servings

Preparation Time: 1 Hour

List of Ingredients:

- 4 Potatoes, Baking Variety and Cut into Half Slices
- ¼ Cup of Butter, Melted
- 8 Slices of Bacon, Fully Cooked and Crumbled
- 8 Ounces of Cheddar Cheese, Finely Shredded
- ½ Cup of Onions, Green in Color and Finely Chopped

AAAAAAAAAAAAAAAAAAAAAAAAAAAAAAAAAAAAAAAAAAAAAA

Instructions:

1. The first thing you want to do is preheat your oven to 400 degrees.

2. Then brush both size of your potatoes with some butter and place them onto a generally greased cookie sheet. Place into your oven to bake for the next 30 to 40 minutes or until light brown in color. Remove.

3. Top your potatoes with your remaining ingredients and continue to bake until your cheese has completely melted. Remove and serve right away.

Recipe 20: Bacon and Ranch Pasta Salad

Here is another great tasting dish that you can bring with you to your next family gathering. The bacon that you will use in this recipe helps to give it a unique flavor that you will fall in love with. It is light and healthy to taste.

Serving Sizes: 10 Servings

Preparation Time: 1 Hour and 25 Minutes

List of Ingredients:

- 1 Pack of Rotini Pasta, Uncooked and Tri-Colored
- 10 Slices of Bacon, Thick Cut
- 1 Cup of Mayo, Your Favorite Kind
- 3 Tablespoons of Ranch Salad Dressing, Dry Mix Variety
- ¼ teaspoons of Garlic, Powdered Variety
- ½ teaspoons of Garlic, Peppered Variety
- ½ Cup of Milk, Whole
- 1 Tomato, Large in Size and Finely Chopped
- 1 Can of Black Olives, Finely Sliced

- 1 Cup of Cheddar Cheese, Sharp Variety and Finely Shredded

AAAAAAAAAAAAAAAAAAAAAAAAAAAAAAAAAAAAAAAAAAAA

Instructions:

1. The first thing you want to do is bring a large size pot of water to a boil over medium to high heat. Once the water is boiling at in your pasta and cook until tender. This should take about 8 minutes.

2. Next place your bacon into a large sized skillet place over medium to high heat and cook until brown in color. Once browned remove and drain on a plate lined with paper towels. Once cooled, crumble.

3. Then use a large sized bowl and add in your remaining ingredients including your cooked pasta. Stir to thoroughly combine. Cover with some plastic wrap and place into your fridge to chill for at least one hour.

4. If your pasta salad is a little dry, feel free to add some more milk until the desired wetness.

Recipe 21: Bacon Wrapped Hamburgers

If you are looking for the most delicious burger recipe that you will ever come across, then this is the perfect hamburger recipe for you. Regardless of how you like your burgers, these burgers always come out extremely tender.

Serving Sizes: 6 Servings

Preparation Time: 25 Minutes

List of Ingredients:

- ½ Cup of Cheddar Cheese, Finely Shredded
- 1 tablespoon of Parmesan Cheese, Finely Grated
- 1 Onion, Small in Size and Finely Chopped
- 1 Egg, Large in Size and Beaten Slightly
- 1 tablespoon of Ketchup, Your Favorite Kind
- 1 tablespoon of Worcestershire Sauce
- ½ teaspoons of Salt, For Taste
- 1/8 teaspoons of Pepper, For Taste
- 1 Pound of Beef, Ground and Lean
- 6 Slices of Bacon, Thick Cut

- 6 Hamburger Buns, Evenly Split

AAAAAAAAAAAAAAAAAAAAAAAAAAAAAAAAAAAAAAAAAAAA

Instructions:

1. First preheat your grill to high heat.

2. While your grill is heating up use a large sized bowl and combine all of your ingredients together except for your bacon until you have a thick patty mixture on your hands.

3. Use your hands and make 6 patties. Then wrap a slice of bacon around each one and secure with a toothpick.

4. Place your patties onto your hot grill and cook for at least 5 minutes on each side or until well done. Remove and serve on hamburger buns. Enjoy.

Recipe 22: Classic Chicken and Bacon Shish Kabobs

This grilled dish makes the tangiest and marinated chicken kabobs. These are the perfect treats to make when you want to make a dish to entertain all of your guests.

Serving Sizes: 6 Servings

Preparation Time: 1 Hour and 45 Minutes

List of Ingredients:

- ¼ Cup of Soy Sauce, Your Favorite Kind
- ¼ Cup of Vinegar, Cider Variety
- 2 Tablespoons of Honey, Raw
- 2 Tablespoons of Oil, Canola Variety
- 10 Mushrooms, Large in Size and Sliced in Half
- 2 Onions, Green in Color and Minced
- 3 Chicken Breasts, Skinless, Boneless and Cut into Small Pieces
- ½ Pound of Bacon, Thick Cut and Sliced in Half
- 1 Can of Pineapple, Chunks, Drained
- A Few Skewers

Instructions:

1. Use a large sized bowl and mix together your first five ingredients until thoroughly mixed. Then add in your mushrooms and chicken and stir thoroughly to combine. Cover with some plastic wrap and marinate in your fridge for the next hour.

2. Then preheat your grill over high heat.

3. Remove your chicken and mushrooms from your marinade and make sure to shake off any excess marinade. Then pour your marinade into a small sized saucepan and bring your mixture to a boil over high heat. Once boiling reduce your heat to low and cook for the next 10 minutes. Remove from heat and set aside.

4. Wrap up your chicken with slices of bacon and thread onto metal skewers until each is secured. Make sure to alternate your mushrooms and pineapples slices throughout your kabobs.

5. Then lightly grease your grill with some oil and place your kabobs on top. Cook for the next 15 to 20 minutes, making sure to brush with your marinade. Cook until your bacon is crispy and your chicken is thoroughly cooked through. Remove and serve right away.

Recipe 23: Healthy BLT Salad

Here is yet another BLT inspired recipe that I know you are going to love. It is yet another healthy salad recipe that you can enjoy during the hot summer months.

Serving Sizes: 6 Servings

Preparation Time: 25 Minutes

List of Ingredients:

- 1 Pound of Bacon, Thick Cut
- ¾ Cup of Mayo, Your Favorite Kind
- ¼ Cup of Milk, Whole
- 1 teaspoon of Garlic Powder
- 1/8 teaspoons of Black Pepper, For Taste
- Dash of Salt, For Taste
- 1 Head of Lettuce, Romaine Variety, Rinsed, Dried and Roughly Shredded
- 2 Tomatoes, Large in Size and Finely Chopped
- 2 Cups of Croutons, Seasoned Variety

AAAAAAAAAAAAAAAAAAAAAAAAAAAAAAAAAAAAAAAAAAAAAA

Instructions:

1. Then cook your bacon in a large sized skillet place over medium to high heat. Cook until thoroughly brown in color. Once browned remove and drain on a plate lined with paper towels. Once cooled, crumble.

2. Then use a food processor and combine your next 4 ingredients together. Blend on the highest setting until smooth consistency. Season with a dash of salt.

3. Then combine your remaining ingredients together in a large sized salad bowl including your cooked bacon. Toss with your pre-made dressing and serve right away. Enjoy.

Recipe 24: Delicious BLT Dip

If you are a huge fan of classic BLT sandwiches, then this is one dip recipe that you will definitely want to make for yourself. It will become a huge hit at your next block party or dinner party. Feel free to use low fat or fat free ingredients to make this dish healthier for you and your guests.

Serving Sizes: 16 Servings

Preparation Time: 25 Minutes

List of Ingredients:

- 1 Pound of Bacon, Thick Cut
- 1 Cup of Mayo, Your Favorite Kind
- 1 Cup of Sour Cream
- 1 Tomato, Large in Size, Peeled, Seeded and Finely Diced

AAAAAAAAAAAAAAAAAAAAAAAAAAAAAAAAAAAAAAAAAAAAAA

Instructions:

1. Then cook your bacon in a large sized skillet place over medium to high heat. Cook until thoroughly brown in color. Once browned remove and drain on a plate lined with paper towels. Once cooled, crumble.

2. Use a medium sized bowl and combine your mayo and sour cream together until evenly mixed. Then add in your crumbled bacon and stir again to combine. Last add in your tomatoes and serve right away. Enjoy.

Recipe 25: Delicious Bacon and Cheddar Deviled Eggs

If you are a huge fan of deviled eggs, then I now you are going to love this recipe. These eggs are actually much better than your traditional deviled eggs and will make a treat that you will want to make over and over again.

Serving Sizes: 12 Servings

Preparation Time: 40 Minutes

List of Ingredients:

- 12 Eggs, Large in Size
- ½ Cup of Mayo, Your Favorite Kind
- 4 Slices of Bacon, Thick Cut
- 2 Tablespoons of Cheddar Cheese, Finely Shredded
- 1 tablespoon of Mustard

AAAAAAAAAAAAAAAAAAAAAAAAAAAAAAAAAAAAAAAAAAAAAAAA

Instructions:

1. The first thing you want to do is place your eggs into a small sized saucepan and cover with some water. Bring the water to a boil and then immediately remove from heat. Cover and allow your eggs to cook in the hot water for the next 10 to 12 minutes. After this time remove from the water and cool under some running water. Set aside.

2. Then cook your bacon in a large sized skillet place over medium to high heat. Cook until thoroughly brown in color. Once browned remove and drain on a plate lined with paper towels. Once cooled, crumble.

3. Next peel your hard boiled eggs and cut in half lengthwise. Scoop out your yolks into a small size bowl and then mash the yolks with your mayo, cooked bacon, and cheese. Stir in your mustard and stir to combine. Fill each of your egg white halves with your yolk mixture and place into your fridge to chill until you are ready to serve.

About the Author

Molly Mills always knew she wanted to feed people delicious food for a living. Being the oldest child with three younger brothers, Molly learned to prepare meals at an early age to help out her busy parents. She just seemed to know what spice went with which meat and how to make sauces that would dress up the blandest of pastas. Her creativity in the kitchen was a blessing to a family where money was tight and making new meals every day was a challenge.

Molly was also a gifted athlete as well as chef and secured a Lacrosse scholarship to Syracuse University. This was a blessing to her family as she was the first to go to college and at little cost to her parents. She took full advantage of her college education and earned a business degree. When she graduated, she joined her culinary skills and business acumen into a successful catering business. She wrote her first e-book after a customer asked if she could pay for several of her recipes. This sparked the entrepreneurial spirit in Mills and she thought if one person wanted them, then why not share the recipes with the world!

Molly lives near her family's home with her husband and three children and still cooks for her family every chance she gets. She plays Lacrosse with a local team made up of her old teammates from college and there are always some tasty nibbles on the ready after each game.

Don't Miss Out!

Scan the QR-Code below and you can sign up to receive emails whenever Molly Mills publishes a new book. There's no charge and no obligation.

Sign Me Up

https://molly.gr8.com

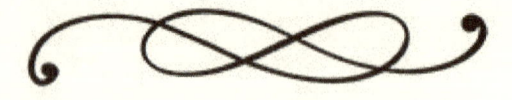